Knots

The Lifeline of Emotions

Hina Beg

BookLeaf Publishing

India | USA | UK

Dedication

In loving memory of my father, the late Dr. M. U. Beg, whose wisdom and love continue to guide me.

For my mother, Naheed Umair, whose nurturing spirit has shaped who I am.

And to all my loved ones, whose support weaves the threads of my journey through life.

Acknowledgements

As I embark on the journey of penning words into poetry in 'Knots: The Lifeline of Emotions', I want to express my heartfelt gratitude to those who have shaped my path.

To my clients, thank you for your trust and openness. Your courage in navigating life's challenges continually inspires me. Each story you've shared has deepened my understanding of resilience and the human spirit, weaving itself into this collection.

To my husband, Farid Khan, thank you for believing in my voice and encouraging me to explore the depths of my thoughts and emotions. Your unwavering support has made this endeavour possible.

To my children, Hiba, Abdul and Faiz, your laughter and curiosity inspire me every day. You show me the beauty in simplicity and the strength that comes from our connections.

To my siblings, Uzma Khan and Mansoor Beg, thank you for being my unwavering pillars of support. Your love and encouragement have guided me on my journey, and I am truly grateful for your willingness to always listen.

And to my readers, thank you for embarking on this journey with me. Your willingness to explore the complexities of life gives purpose to my words.

This collection reflects the experiences we've shared as a family and the lessons learned through my work with clients. May it serve as a testament to the resilience and love that bind us all.

Thank you, everyone, for being my constant source of strength.

Preface

Life is a tapestry of tangled threads, each representing moments, emotions and connections.

In 'Knots: The Lifeline of Emotions', I invite you to journey through the intricate maze of human experience. This collection of poems delves into the feelings that bind us – embracing both the depths of pain and the heights of joy, as well as the complexities of relationships and the resilience that lies within us all.

As a therapist, my hope is that these verses provide not only solace but also motivation. The struggles of this generation are great, yet I believe that each individual is blessed in countless ways and possesses the strength to keep moving forward.

Each poem serves as a mirror reflecting our shared humanity, capturing echoes of care and the weight of modern life. In a world where emotions can feel overwhelming, I hope these verses resonate and remind you that you are not alone in this struggle.

As I often say, 'When you are tough, nothing will be easy. Be prepared!' Life is filled with knots that we tie through our experiences, but remember: opening those knots can bring relief. The process of unravelling what binds us allows space for healing and growth.

From the everyday pressures that weigh heavily on our shoulders to the fleeting moments of joy that uplift our spirits, this collection illuminates the beauty found within the knots we navigate and the freedom that comes when we learn to open them.

Thank you for joining me on this journey. May you discover strength, connection and a touch of light as you navigate your own tapestry of life.

Table of Contents

Fragments of Humanity

Right now, the world is cool with chaos,
To test my learning in a practical way.
I live to try and never give up–
Is this enough to be happy and say:
Finally, I am at peace!

Halt! There is chaotic calmness within.
Moments rushing and crisscrossing our hearts,
Only to surprise the logical mind–
That nothing comes easy, no matter what we part.

The fragments of thoughts
Try desperately to make sense.
Is there anymore humanity
As we chatter behind a fragile fence?

History chuckles and quietly breathes;
The red grass, with time, slowly decays.
Enough time given to human beings,
The bots laughed, and we were only in prayers.

Echoes of Care

The whistle that blew out of nowhere
Is a reminder of people who truly care.
Oblivious to the fact that the alarm is there
To remind you and make you aware.

The changes in life are in a hurry;
You will notice only when you worry.
So just sit down for now on a dhurrie,
And why not enjoy your hot curry?

Gratitude is there for each one of you,
To make my life easier as I grew,
Being there and seeing my journey through–
The roller coaster of moments that just flew.

It's time to say what is right,
As darkness looms, the night is bright.
I care and will bounce back with my might;
Just let me doze off without a fight.

The Journey Within

Our minds can weave a complex plan,
Spinning thoughts, we think we can.
Little do we know, it's not so easy,
Turning dreams into actions can make us dizzy.

Desires amplified by imagination's fire,
Social media stokes the burning desire.
Nothing's impossible, we give it a try,
Yet failure lingers, no matter how we cry.

Silent tears streak down our face,
We breathe in sobs as our hearts race.
But we'll rise again, ready for the chase;
Hope lifts our spirits, guiding with grace.

Go slow with the plan, that's what I say,
Don't hesitate too long; keep moving away.
Through hardship's rhythm, let your heart play,
A new chapter unfolds, and you'll find your way.

Efforts shine bright, reflecting a smile,
Look at your journey; you've travelled each mile.
Though it was tough, your grit grew all the while,
Now pause and enjoy life, in your OG style...

Voice of a Child

Something dropped, and my heart pounded,
I rushed to the room, utterly astounded,
To see my princess cleaning the mess–
Just innocent pieces of chess.

Her smile was contagious, and I laughed,
She left the room with her red scarf.
I sat there, picking up the pieces,
While she jumps and skips, her energy never
ceases.

Children need time; it's all they ask,
Parents should listen, not consider it a task.
Their nonstop babble, a joyous utter,
As they enjoy bread, jam and butter.

Munching on goodies, they're in a good mood,
All they need is love – it's simple and crude.
So let's slow down and relish the day,
For their sweet talk is pure, a stress antidote, they
say.

Listen to the voices that scream and cry,
Do they need anything before you pry?
Innocence is torn by the confusion around,

Will happiness linger, or is it lost, never found?

Relax and breathe as you hold your child,
Nothing is needed; this thought is not wild.
The time you give to join in their play
Is precious for them and will forever stay.

Deep down, you give them something to hold,
As they grow up, they'll cherish it bold.
Let them make messes with toys or clay;
May they grow to be good humans – is all we may
pray.

So be warm and soothing to your child's voice,
Be their role model, mentor – let them rejoice.

Joyful Ironies

Laughter can cry,
Breaking silence with noisy whispers,
Capturing moments while we roam free,
Catching lies like a truthful thief.

Sometimes it's fine to be awfully good;
This is reality, a secret that's understood.
We overlook the small crowd's parade,
Doing the same thing in a grand charade.

It's odd how we misunderstood the plot,
Cruising through life with joyful regret.
Picking up pace in a hurried crawl,
Cracking up silently, wise fools enthral.

As old news resurfaces, fresh and stale,
Everything we knew tells a comical tale.
Now it all seems seriously funny,
The drama of goals – a working vacation, sunny.

Monday's Comfy Conquest

Oh, Monday is here, the sneaky little beast,
Knocking with a coffee and a workday feast.
Alarm clocks blaring bring a wake-up surprise;
Why is it always you that brings sleepy eyes?

My to-do list grows like a weed in spring,
With tasks that feel like a game in a ring.
Emails pile up like laundry in a heap,
And I dream of a world where we all extend our
sleep.

I spill my coffee, a splash on my shirt–
A fashion statement? Or just plain dirt?
Meetings are endless, with chatter and sighs,
As I nod and pretend I'm oh-so-wise.

But now I'm at home, in my comfy chair,
Trading office chaos for cosy flair.
No more cubicles, just my cat and tea,
Skipping the mundane – it's pure glee, you see!

So here's to Mondays, you lovable prank;
You fill our lives with your work, to be frank.

We may groan and moan as the week starts anew,
But from home with a smile, we'll conquer, it's
true!

People of Today

Is it this life we are craving for?
When they have everything yet want much more,
Crushing the less privileged under their paw–
Nature will shriek and say, 'I saw!'

People feel content by destroying others' share;
What others feel is what they least care.
They don't understand that their species is rare,
But to challenge each other is what they dare.

For money's sake, soft hearts have grown stoned,
Killing and torturing even those they've known.
Seeing everyone so selfish makes me feel alone–
When such people perish, will anyone really
mourn?

Young Teenager

Hey there, friends! Don't be aghast if you don't
see yourself in me.
I'm the new young teenager, just a tad over forty–
What? Aah, save that for yourself!
At this age, hormones throw a party,
And everyone's reacting like it's a tragedy!

We're juggling life like circus acts,
Throwing tantrums while we're still young at
heart–
Hormones creating chaos; it's an art!
The changes are wild, and we're feeling the
impact,
Responsibilities piling up – oh, where's our snack?

Age is like sand, slipping through our hands,
Clapping along with grand moments and plans.
Life has been a blast, but this teenage vibe?
Not quite what we wanted; it's a bumpy ride.
Coping with changes while caring for the old,
Kids on the edge, and we're losing our gold.

No time to laugh, and enjoy that's carefree,
Hormones having a ball while we're their
marquee.

This is the most demanding phase of our life,
A rollercoaster ride – oh, where's the respite?
Real youth, take notice – come and see!
Can you bring some calm to teens like me?

We need a dose of comfort and rest,
Emotional, mental, physical – let's do our best!
After all, we're the young teenagers today,
Full of wisdom, spirit and bright rays.
Cheer up! The aches are here to stay–
Let's meet at the gym, come on, let's slay–
And afterwards, we'll sip coffee and laugh the day
away!

Coping Hacks

Those words hurt when they talk about me,
How much more can I truly bear?
Every conversation steals my glee–
When will this end? I just sit and stare.

The words shoot at me from all around,
My screams echo in a silent vacuum.
Thoughts buried deep, nowhere to be found,
In a world where many feel the same gloom.

Emotions tossed, baked or fried,
My heart aches for each soul in dismay.
I offer my tips, hoping they'll guide–
Living in the moment is the mantra today.

Build yourself like never before;
Let emotions empower, lift your true core.
Believing isn't easy, but trust in what's sure–
Redefine yourself for the moments in store.

Your chatter matters; that much is true–
Life hacks help you learn to glow.
Your path is lit; you're the GOAT, it's you!
Living with focus will help you grow.

So who else needs these coping skills?
Step right up, don't hesitate, just shine.
Together we'll navigate life's uphill thrills–
Embrace the journey, and everything will align.

Pressure

'There is work to do' – a common phrase,
As people fixate on the tasks at hand,
Seldom pausing to find praise
For what they've achieved, the progress so grand.

So consumed by their relentless grind,
The pressure builds within their hearts.
Hardly noticing the hurdles left behind,
The joy they miss, a distant art.

This pressure, unknown to its master,
Encroaches on body and soul.
When to relax feels like a disaster–
Is this life plan clear, or just a toll?

Technology races at a dizzying pace,
Creating FOMO in our crowded minds.
Days grow shorter, with no end in place–
Will we realise this chaos we find?

The pressure tests our very limits,
Forcing us to prepare,
To be replaced by bots,
As we waste time without a care.

A self-dug grave of chaos and pain,
The harsh reality of today.
Will we take onus, or let pressure reign,
And watch our joys slowly fade away?

Wake up before you complain;
Time is still on your side.
Embrace the pressure in your life,
Breathe deep, and let joy be your guide.

In challenges, find a dance,
Where pressure melts into grace.
Connect with the rhythm, take a chance,
And let your spirit find its place.

As you weave through this vibrant maze,
Pressure transforms into gentle flow.
Embrace the dream, let colours blaze,
And watch your heart's true journey grow.

Pain

It hurts to see such pain,
When life itself is in strain.
Everyone busy as a bee,
Chasing security, love, money and health–
But alas, it all depends on wealth.

Death is certain from the moment we're born,
Yet emotions and wisdom are ground and torn,
To pieces that, if we want to feel,
We can hear, smell or bury with a seal.

Humanity exists, but attitudes change,
Hierarchy looms, yet feels so strange–
No one approves, yet here they're trapped,
In careers or idleness, a puzzling riddle wrapped.

A lingering pain shatters the air,
Words that once flowed now vanish in despair,
As heartbeats fade, leaving trails of mourn,
Memories echo, bittersweet and worn.

The end of one is a new beginning;
Live well, be true, embrace the living.
You never know who's next in the queue,
So be happy, be kind and be true.

Laughter and harmony heal that pain,
A balm that will surely never go in vain!

Depth of a Survivor

The look in an eye
Could be genuine or shy.
The smile on a face
Simple, yet filled with grace.

The touch of a hand
Can be soft or sand.
The feelings of a soul
Can be at the equator or the pole.

The message of a mind
Can be calming or refined.
The meaning of a survivor
Is either stagnant or a driver.

Through trials they rise,
With courage that defies.
Each scar tells a tale,
Of strength that won't pale.

Aching Feelings

There are feelings in my body
That brings a heavy pain.
I know that the one I've lost
Will never return again.

Grief weaves a complex tapestry,
Each thread a lingering ache.
The harmony of life feels shattered,
As I navigate this fragile state.

A tear-streaked face reflects the struggle,
A silent, haunting guest.
Though I wrestle with the sorrow,
It's part of the heart's relentless quest.

I seek solace in quiet moments,
Embracing thoughts that run deep.
Knowing others share this burden,
And also yearn for peace and sleep.

The lump in my throat,
A constant reminder of loss,
Yet within this weighty silence,
I find strength in what it costs.

There are feelings in my body
That pulse with vibrant life;
They ache and spark warmth in memory,
As I embrace the balance of joy and strife.

Theory of Mind

Look! You are bound to collide,
Neglect, and you will collide.
Collision is a theory,
Fiery and often weary.
It makes us ponder
How all matters wander.

People meet and depart,
Yet never forget from the heart–
How, when and where they met,
Creating bonds we can't forget.

'Live and let live' is seldom seen;
People wary of the present scene.
Happiness is rare in daily life,
Often found between husband and wife.
While others wield a knife,
Taking from others in their usual stride.

Smiles have lost their authenticity,
Only found in a hallucinated city.
Living in dreams can feel so bright,
But to survive, one must find the light.

It's a deep thought our minds have caught;

Give some time to your little mind,
And you will see that life can be kind.

Gist of Reality

Life can feel exotically suffocating,
As humanity is always creating,
Never realising their true need,
Destroying what's vital for every breed.

Fresh air is no longer pure;
Prevention is known to be better than cure.
Yet it's sad to see this modern era,
Empowering the innocent with its terror.

Trees are cut for furniture or fire;
Everything's in a crux to feed our pyre.
The vicious cycle of need, want and desire,
Brings fleeting joy but can also tire.

What a hypothetical way to live,
Where we take much more than we give.
How I wish people could be caring,
Recognising that the end is nearing.

Hope that all may live with genuine fun–
Then they'll be amazed by what can be done.
So let us live and not deprive,
For everyone deserves the right to survive!

Call to Self

I wake up to my chaotic self,
All my plans for coffee tossed on the shelf.
When did I snooze the alarm? I wonder–
In a jiffy, I'm ready; no time to ponder.

Honking and loud noise hit me hard,
But who cares? This thought I quickly discard.
Catching my train is all that matters,
The buzz around me, just mere chatter.

The wheels move slowly, a soothing balm,
I breathe in rhythm, finding my calm.
Looking around, I see the same game,
Everyone's in this; no one to blame.

I pause this self-pity trip,
Smile at a lady with a cane and a grip.
Her face beams back; I feel instant glee,
In that small moment, I'm happy, you see.

As I enter my workplace with a smile,
People glance at me for a while.
'What happened?' they ask, wide-eyed and keen,
In this halo of happiness, I bask like a queen.

With a mountain of work still to do,
Throughout the day, I smile, my focus true.
Finishing tasks with an unknown joy–
Oh, life is simple; I toy with this ploy.

Strangely today, I went to the gym,
Something inside compelled me to begin.
Fitness and self-care are not to deny,
A promise to myself that I will try.

Enough is enough; I make a vow,
No matter what comes, I won't bow.
Life is a roller coaster ride,
And I'll cruise through it with my stride.

How blessed am I to miss that coffee?
For nothing in life comes free, you see.
My new look is one I proudly own–
Finally, my heart whispers, 'Oh, I have grown'!

Shadows of Comparison

Oh, how hard I've tried to make this right,
Yet you say it's simply not enough.
Look over there – see their flawless might,
How effortlessly they work, leaving nothing
rough.

I turn away with a casual glance;
What can change this? I already know.
Thoughts freeze in a nervous dance,
As their brilliance shines, leaving me feeling low.

Avoiding the gaze that weighs like a stone,
Unaware of the battles I've faced alone.
Words fly like arrows, harsh and unkind,
Leaving me silent, lost in the tone.

My cherished ideas met with scorn,
Emotions sinking, a heavy shroud.
Confidence trampled, my spirit worn–
Will I ever rise from this oppressive crowd?

Then a child appeared, with a voice so bright,
'Look how lovely you are in that shade of red!'
In a flash, they sparked my fading light,
And dashed away, leaving joy instead.

I searched for the source of this gentle lift,
The reminder that kindness can still exist.
People can pause, their hearts can shift–
The onus is on me to find my bliss.

Comparison lurks in every life's game,
Ready to challenge, ready to steal.
Whether student, partner or bearing a name,
No one can hinder my own inner zeal.

Believe in yourself; it's the treasure you own–
Skills and wisdom are yours to share.
Trust the journey of how far you've grown;
Embrace life's peace – let go of despair.

Each has their path, their trials to bear,
With their hopes, their dreams and will.
Now I breathe deeply, knowing I'm rare–
Did I just compare what I sought to kill?

All They Say!

'Eat fruits and see your skin glow,'
'I'm munching on nuts – am I going nuts?' I
throw.
'Don't be an idiot,' is all they say,
'Wake up early and start your day.'
'But I work night shifts,' I quietly convey.
'You have a job – be grateful,' is all they say.

Children head to school with bags so big,
I look surprised; with tuition packed in, what a
gig.
'This is a must, you dumb,' is all they say.
Teaching us to talk, yet quieting our play.
'When will you understand?' is all they say.

Learning to walk with those baby steps known,
Now roaming with friends, acting all grown.
'You hardly sit with us,' is all they say.
I try to be present, my phone tucked away,
Yet lo and behold, they have more to convey.
'It's our fault to pamper you,' is all they say.

Surprised at the words they choose,
Feeling desperate to leave, as we muse.
'What's bothering you?' is all they say.

I wrote them a letter some time back,
'Let's be a family, and we'll be on track'.
'Hmmm' is all they say.

Surprised by the impact my words had on them,
Never seen them smile; morning joy is rare, a gem.
'You're right, my child,' is all they say.
Since then, I've tried to engage,
Balancing life as they navigate their age.
'I love you' is all they say.

I look around the house, a tear on my face,
'Have I rushed through life, lost in my pace'?
Now no one to say, 'What's wrong?' is all I say

What a Plight

Tigers caged, horses slaved,
Fishes fried, shells dried.
Dogs tied, bees cried,
Man lied, evidence denied.
Danger sign, humans assigned,
Ambitious nature, destroying future.
Species extinct, stupidity winked–
History repeats; prepare at least!

Just a Hope

What is it that wants me to cry
When all I have done is to try?
I feel inside me a heavy pain;
It makes me normal yet insane.

The tears inside my half-droopy eye
Are solidified, except for a dry sigh.
There is only one soul who tried knowing me–
That's a pearl who sets my mind free.

What is it that makes me so numb
When I can't say because of a lump?
I feel around me a lonely air;
It makes me sober and makes me stare.

The world outside my half-opened eye
Is indifferent to what I spy.
There is one hope that I want to see–
That's a simple joy when peace knows me.

Live

Live each and every day,
And learn how to play,
With happiness in your heart,
Oh, what a wonderful way!

Jump for joy and have some fun,
Hop with zeal, let your spirit run,
Rejoice in every little pun,
And exclaim, 'What a glorious sun'!

People will gaze and wonder why,
Some may feel a twinge of envy, oh my!
But those who are genuine, it's true,
Will celebrate your happiness too.

Never let sadness take its hold,
While the world around you grows old.
With a hint of madness, don't be afraid–
Embrace the peace, let worries fade.

Life's too short to let it go to waste,
So shower love with heartfelt haste.
Smile wide, let your laughter be graced,
And savour each moment with a sweet taste.

Finding My Light

Crap I write,
Just to fight.
The confusion within me,
And let myself be free.

This task is hard,
My feelings have no guard.
To nature, they open,
No coupons are needed, just hope in.

I wish for inner solace,
With dignity and grace,
To present myself with a smile,
And keep sadness in a file.

So I sit down and pray,
For warmth to light my way.
To be happy today, tomorrow and forever—
With strength, wisdom and no fear, I'll endeavour.

Journey of Emotions

Today I left my cherished home,
With hopes and dreams, I felt alone.
My parents waved, my sister sighed,
With every step, I felt the tide.

As the wheels began to turn,
A mix of dread and excitement burned.
Will I see my loved ones soon?
This thought hangs heavy like a tune.

The train rolled on from stop to stop,
Strangers chatting, time seemed to hop.
Each face a story, each voice a song,
Yet my heart whispers where I belong.

My destination draws near, yet I fear,
This path is bright but also unclear.
For studies' sake, I must be brave,
But leaving home feels like a wave.

We must work hard and find our way,
That's the message I need to say.
Those who drift may come to know,
How precious the roots that help us grow.

The Burden of a Student's Heart

Light flickered and darkness engulfed me
I was so lonely that I could hardly see,
Absorbing the moment as my heart raced,
Jogging my emotions at a dull pace.
Sitting in my room with loads of books,
Portions to complete– in this cycle, I am hooked.
It was a tough call to make,
When my parents' expectations were at stake.

They never said in so many words,
My likings ignored and they hardly heard.
The silent love for other things–
This, with time, they said, will sink.
I switched to the current mode,
Did my best and aced the boards.
With each passing day, I tried;
Deep within me, my heart cried.

I wanted to cope with everyone around,
The energy alone which I never found.
I smiled and laughed with others in class,
But slowly I found it difficult to pass.
This was not me, I could see it through;

'It's okay, next time you will pass, beta,' they
knew.
I collected myself with new vigour—
Again, the speed and portion were the trigger.

I failed to hold on as I screamed,
'Wish they could see' is all I dreamed.
Life seemed meaningless as I dipped so low,
That I became more and more slow.
About to end this mayhem within,
I decided to give up without feeling any sin.
All set to go, and then I came to know
A new teacher had come and was asking me to
show.

I dragged myself to the room upstairs,
All I could do was just stand and stare.
Her soft voice was hard to miss;
Is this the moment where life was bliss?
She made me sit and gave me water–
This gesture moved me, and I wanted to chatter.
Tears escaped quietly as I saw her there;
Something within urged me to share.

My emotions were charred with so much weight;
She just then asked, 'When was the last time I
ate'?
How did she know I skipped my meals?

Was I worth knowing, or was this my parents'
deal?
Slowly, as it dawned that she was with me,
I felt at ease, and the bigger picture I could see.
She was the therapist in the hostel to stay,
To listen, know, guide and light the way.

To all those who are battling with pressure and
pain,
I would suggest try sharing, which will not go in
vain.
It's true life is tough and difficult to understand,
But you are tougher and have the grit to
command.
The nuances of challenges thrown your way
Will be handled with calmness, like a child's play.
Never give up hope,
As life is all about how you cope!

Dad Jokes and the Morning Madness

Every day is an adventure with my dad around,
Leaving no stone unturned to wake me from the
ground.
'Look at the time! You're always late!'
I grab my phone – wait, it's not even eight!

With a soft voice, I murmur, 'Five minutes more',
He stands by the clock, ready to roar.
'Five minutes over – now get up and eat!'
He rushes off to whip up a morning treat.

Still dazed, I wonder, where am I?
Before I can think, comes a loud cry,
'Are you ready, kids of today?'
He mumbles it all in a single say.

I jump out of bed at the sound of his word,
Knowing his tone is sharper than a sword.
'Why do nights end so soon'?
What is the hurry, dear Mr. Moon?

'Still not ready?' my father said,
His tone caught my ear; I sprang from my bed.

Something was bothering him, I could see,
I peeked into the kitchen and just found tea.

'What happened to the toast'? I wondered aloud,
Suddenly, breakfast didn't seem to make me
proud.
A burning smell wafted from behind the door–
What else could I ask for, nothing more?

My dear father, the master cook,
Thought he'd whip up a feast with his phone as a
book.
Caught up in reels, he lost track of the smoke,
Coughing and choking – a humorous joke!

No more loud voice thrown my way,
I helped him clean up before Mom could say.
He smiled softly and gently said,
'Dear son, you can go back to bed.'

Surprised by his words, I raised an eyebrow,
'Today's Sunday,' he said, taking a bow.
So here's to the chaos and laughter we share,
In the journey of fatherhood, I'm grateful you're
always there!

Few Lines from Within

Why do people have emotions?
Where do they originate?
Is it only for certain notions,
Or is it written in one's fate?

Why do people have feelings?
Where are they born?
Do they shift with every dealing,
Or remain the same from each dawn?

Why don't people just laugh it off?
Where are their brains?
They cry over socks gone missing–
Leading to drama, chaos and pain!!

Why don't people cool down and live?
Where are they headed with every try?
Why can't they find joy in what they give,
Since empty-handed they came and so will they
die!

Joy of a Cancelled Lecture

Why are you up so late? my mother inquired,
'I have an assignment to submit', I said, tired.
Inside my mind, I knew if it wasn't done, I'd be
fired,
Thoughts churned like a blender – this was no
fun!

The phone vibrated frantically; I could see,
No time to talk, I sighed in tension – like a bee!
'Pick up your phone,' my soul whispered, 'take a
moment free!'
I answered the call, curiosity had me on a spree.

'Finished?' was the new hello,
'What? Not yet?' I could only say.
'No way!' was the surprised echo–
'Chill! Just complete it', I silently prayed.

As I spoke, two new missed calls chimed in,
'Why is everyone panicking'? I wondered with a
grin.
Tried to join them to chat about football's spin,

But was silenced, pondering – where did my time
begin?

Back to my work, the clock ticked away,
Gaining speed like a hamster on a wheel, hooray!
Soon I munched everything that came my way,
Alas, I finished my work, with a side of play.

Is that my mom's alarm or am I dreaming?
Suddenly I perspired; the fan was off, oh
gleaming!
This is reality, I sat with sun beaming,
Submission dawned on me; my heart was
screaming.

Checked my phone – twenty missed calls?
Skipping a beat, I called back with my woes.
The group call connected, football talk enthrals.
Dazed at the change from what to how it flows.

'You don't know?' was the new hello,
Accepting my ignorance, I laughed – oh no!
'Lecture cancelled!' they cheered, in unison, a
show,
My body supercharged with joy—like a puppy in
tow.

In no moment, eager to go to college,

As my favourite spot awaited, it was time to
acknowledge.
Quickly, we all were on the edge,
Kicking the ball on the ground – a joyous pledge!

Silent Blow

Health is wealth, so they say.
It's at a price, so they pray.
Leaving the needy – at bay,
Comfort for comfortable, so let us slay.

Crying out loud, no voice is heard,
The ears so safe, that's hard to break.
The heart sealed – with mind blocked,
Life screamed, halted and shocked!

They speak of change, yet words are free–
A world built on shadows, blind to see.
Riches flow, while hunger grows,
A silent storm, no one knows.

Faces turn, and hands retract,
Promises made, but none intact.
The weak remain beneath the tide,
Silent in their tears, they hide.

A candle flickers, its light so dim,
A life denied its every whim.
The affluent feast, yet still they crave–
While the desperate crowd by the grave.

Hands stretched out, but none to hold,
The story of the voiceless, untold.
Comfort is a fortress, tall and wide,
Where the cries of the fallen collide.

Yet through the silence, whispers rise—
A distant plea beneath the skies.
A question hangs, unspoken, bare—
Who will listen? Who will care?

The Speed of Emotion!!

Where have we come as a nation?
A burning topic, with burning hearts, misted
eyes.
Those who deny the situation–
I wonder, do they follow any religion?
Every moment, a life is lost,
With wailing relatives and the heavy cost.

How long will we live in this despair?
Is this the nation we are preparing to share?
To the generations struggling, fighting hard,
Trying to make sense, discarding the scars.
Hopelessness creeps in, and negative vibes,
Can we just STOP all the endless jibes?

Humaneness is shrinking,
Ignorance, bold and winking.
It's high time we all UNITE,
To voice against the darkness and fight.

My impromptu feelings I share,
In this fleeting moment, I spare...
Let's bow our heads and pray,
For the broken, the lost, in every way.
And in this prayer, humanity is found,

A spark of hope, where love abounds.

Personal Growth, Self-Improvement and Resilience

Quotes focusing on self-development, personal growth, resilience and overcoming challenges.

1. Relive your passion. Do not let the moments stagnate
2. Your focus may sway at times from your lit path. Be vigil
3. Hope is the heartbeat of resilience, echoing louder with every act of kindness and courage
4. Holding on to a ray of hope is enough to melt down any frozen heart
5. Stop comparing. Explore creativity
6. Stop looking for an easy life. Ignite determination
7. Stop striving to be happy all the time. Try contentment
8. Dominate action to defeat self-doubt
9. Surpass the bar of validation
10. Retrieve the power from criticism
11. Dedication: Self-commitment is nurtured by this baseline quality

12. Patience: Relationships and work need you with this attribute

13. Think sincerely about giving up your distractions in pursuit of your dreams

14. Trust your calibre before you quit

15. Believe in yourself before you judge

16. Pain has only one healing language – humanity

17. Procrastination is like quicksand– be cautious

18. Opportunities may come in the form of work or suggestions

19. The right attitude will balance your life, no matter where you are

20. Life is tough and that is a guarantee. But you are tougher, that is the assurance

21. Keep going even if the path is bumpy and dark

22. Blurry vision may decay your mission

23. Standing alone at times is an outstanding achievement

24. Timely shedding away your baggage will beautify your life

25. Journey towards your dream will have dark moments. Just keep moving. Light of confidence will light your way

26. Life may choke you with despair. Your inner grit will help you to grow and repair

27. Helping others to grow does not deplete your individuality

28. Don't crawl if you want to fly. The right
approach is all that matters
29. The hour will come. It's the minutes that count
30. Revitalise your day with bright soothing
moments
31. Half imagination can leave our imagination
dry
32. The consistent efforts never go in vain. Let the
veins carry enthusiasm, positivity and
peace
33. Anger is a powerful tool. It can make or break
you
34. The frozen emotions will take time to thaw,
but once they do – they dissolve beautifully
35. They say never to give up; for me, it is to just
get up. The dreams I aspire, lift me up and
inspire. I set myself free. That is me!
36. Every day is a new beginning. I will rise and
shine. No matter what, I will strive to bloom
in my circumstances, pure and bliss. This is me!
This is who I am
37. The blend of colours reflects Harmony
38. The power to grow lies within, no matter how
sharp your surroundings are
39. Competitions may be tough. The journey may
be rough. So what! I will grow and stay
firm in my goals. Giving space and radiating
positivity. My nature is to give. Do I exist?

Nope! I purely live

40. The path we choose will be lit up with colours. Focus, believe and keep moving

41. If you are not in the moment, the momentum is lost

42. Fight and be confident even if you are at the edge

43. Confidence – rule your own streak

44. Your looks may be unique. But your skills will make an impact

45. Life will play a game of hide and seek. Be patient and progress with a winning streak

46. We are just a speck. It's time to sparkle

47. Brainstorm all actions before giving up. There is always a spark waiting to light up

48. When you are tough, nothing will be easy. Be prepared!

49. Dynamic nature nurtures many colours

50. Face the heat. Grind the memories and embolden your grit

51. Keep your goals high and your efforts highest

52. The world is small if you plan to tread on it with your courage

53. Beat can beat anything. Just never give up its rhythm

54. You are who you are when you have free time

55. Hurdles like pebbles are motivating only if life keeps flowing through them with momentum

Perspective, Decision-Making and Clarity

Quotes about perspective shifts, making thoughtful decisions and finding clarity in the midst of Uncertainty.

1. Decisions act like a curtain raiser for future performance
2. Choice silently offers a platter of options for decision-making
3. To see the change, you have to dive into the pool of change
4. Your glow may dull but not your attitude
5. Make your presence present
6. Lightning lights up the place, despite the deep thunder
7. The moon shines despite the clouds surrounding it
8. The environment we choose will create its own bow wave, only if we move with determination
9. The nature we choose will flow or blow the opportunities in life

10. Vision – do not lose this precious fuel of life,
in the vastness of time and ambience
11. Time stealers are the thieves of happiness. Be
cautious
12. When your path is clear and the sun raises your
spirits, then just go for it. This is the moment to
seize and achieve
13. Please – a word that acts like a conversation
cooler. Use it to chill
14. When you uproot yourself to plant elsewhere,
remember a part of your lineage is in you. Be
responsible
15. Opportunities may come in the form of
routine, grind and rustic look. Keep your doors of
vision open
16. The more you brainstorm, the more ideas will
crop up. Never give up
17. I feel hurt when no one appreciates. Thus,
today I applaud every effort I make
18. I saw my past invading my future and so I
planned to gift myself this present
19. I feel low when I am lost. So I decided to find
myself and rise
20. The moment I jump to capture and relish, no
compromise made to enrich my memory.
Experience in life struck a balance in me. I walk
with elan and that's exactly the way I
want to be

21. Worry is all about time

22. Validation may chain your creativity

23. Humour is the spice of life

24. Silent battle is actually a war within oneself

25. Teachers are like lamps in your journey. The light is now within you

26. Sharpen your mind with colourful streaks

27. Each layer of experience adds value and is delicious to ears, if the tongue and heart are sweet – rest follows

28. Adjusting your focus will give clarity to your vision

29. Moving ahead does not mean you don't stop, it just means to balance a rhythm

30. Be alert. Your melting self will burn you

31. Before jumping to conclusion, be sure of the facts

32. Clarity will come once you focus

33. Learn to change your track on time, so as to keep the momentum going

34. Smiles are priceless. Keep collecting these treasures in your Pandora box

35. It's human nature to track the path on which they travel

36. Do not surprise your efforts by doubting it. Believe and be confident

37. Do not get disturbed by others' viewpoints. What's yours – that is important

38. When twilight pulls the curtain and pins it
with a star, remember hope is always there–
wherever you are!
39. Sometimes you judge and sometimes you are
judged
40. Do not fudge issues in your life

Nature, Energy and Balance

Quotes about balancing life, connecting with nature and staying grounded in the face of challenges.

1. The silent terrain is a treasure of life and survival
2. The calm water is a chamber for depth and experience
3. The cloudy sky is a playground for hide-and-seek
4. Water from that height never fails to serve its purpose. Be thankful
5. Water at this level never fails to hydrate the souls
6. Water at this depth never loses its power to nurture life. Be gracious
7. Be like charismatic water that absorbs chaos and spreads calmness
8. Be like a sturdy mountain that embraces the clouds to nourish the earth
9. Be like tall trees that stay rooted as they shed their burdens

10. The moon slips away quietly, bringing hope. Be enthusiastic

11. The moon smiles with glittering stars unconditionally. Be cheerful

12. The night sky wraps the earth with coolness. Be calm

13. The sun is setting with humility. Be humble

14. The sun is burning with passion. Be vigilant

15. The sunshine is brimming with curiosity. Be ready

16. Connect with energy as you drive your life with every new sunrise

17. Let your emotions blend in harmony to bring peace in life

18. Mood is an internal vibrant language which nurtures our nature

19. Black is the mind charmer. Absorb its clarity

20. Red is life, oozing with energy. Absorb its zing

21. Orange is passion rejuvenated. Absorb its optimism

22. Yellow is charismatic happiness. Absorb its positivity

23. Green is the wizard in your life. Absorb its growth

24. Blue is wisdom with reliability. Absorb its nature

25. Indigo is tranquillity with integrity. Absorb its harmony

26. Violet is creativity with power. Absorb its royalty

27. White is the soul charmer. Absorb its purity

28. Nature will rejuvenate your nature

29. Education will open your doors of understanding

30. Let the assets grow along, with you in peace

31. Valuing your time is being you

32. Comparison with others will drift you away from your goals

33. Blending the flavours will give harmonious aroma

34. In your journey of life, touch people's heart with warmth

35. Life may tear us apart only to check our heart. Be strong! You do have an important part

36. Frozen clarity when thawed will cool the moments

37. Be firm like mountains. Rooted yet touching the sky

38. Life is a journey. Capture good moments

39. The outside nature will test your depth of patience. Be confident and calm

40. Wheels of life will toss and turn. Just maintain your balance

41. Quiet moments before leaving for work will make you calm

42. Challenges may come from any direction.
Tackling them calmly should be your vision
43. Nothing can buy the peace you earn through
charity
44. Harmony with acceptance is the natural order
of life
45. Thunder made its presence and slowly the
clouds wept
46. Your journey will be enriching if you have a
curious nature
47. Shadows change in size and intensity, so do
emotions
48. Staying calm in dark moments will light your
path
49. The ray of hope lingers beyond the shadows of
time
50. The light within is the only light that can
bring sunshine into your life

Health, Well-Being and Mindfulness

*Quotes about maintaining good health, mindfulness
and the importance of well-being.*

1. Eat to Recharge your energy, which will refuel your vision and dreams
2. Exercise to burn calories, feeding your overthinking zone in your mind
3. Hobby is the best survival trick or hack from all the drama in life
4. Life is too short to spend another day without any sport
5. Hectic life with a loop of chores. Plan to distract with life hack – your hobby
6. Sip away the experiences and rejuvenate yourself
7. Poverty knows no age; be mindful
8. Tears: the powerful hydraulic water-power capable of destroying mental will-power
9. Nourish your soul and see the path of life light up with positivity
10. Living in the moment is your biggest survival hack

11. Happiness is a state of being content in the moment

12. When you encounter turbulence in life, just be calm

13. It's okay to cry. Bottling up emotions can increase pain and lead to other issues

14. Fear is a feeling of known and unknown. Be wary, as it can numb the senses

15. Pain knows no caste, creed, colour, gender or boundaries. It is simply painful

16. May Almighty free you from despair, debt, and restlessness

17. May Almighty heal the pain that only you experience silently and bring ease in life

18. Every mind needs a reminder

19. Pause the scroll and own your morning

20. Sometimes we need to pause, reflect and recharge

21. Curling in your own zone does not mean one is always lonely or upset. It means sleep zone. Stop overthinking

22. You may pause in the tunnel of opportunities. Just don't stop!

23. Regular communication will open doors for positivity

24. Emotions are like raindrops, sometimes soothing and at times devastating

25. Hop over hurdles, follow progress

26. Jog off overthinking; follow actions
27. Run away from negativity; follow vision
28. Jump laziness, follow dreams
29. Skip assumptions, follow facts
30. Avoid caustic tinge to experience the zesty nature
31. Let the sound heal the system, not cause tsunami
32. Clean the surface to bring back the shine
33. You need to throw the trash regularly to create space
34. Humour means to hum our way to soothe internal and external ambience.
35. When it comes to safeguarding self, take out me time
36. Do not let temporary relationships scar you permanently
37. Calm minds learn to tame chaotic moments
38. Emotional health is like chips; the more you indulge, the more you're hooked. Change the flavour to keep it fresh
39. Do not use firecrackers inside your mind and heart
40. There is light beyond clouded vision. Be patient
41. Time moves at its pace. Just carry yourself with grace

42. Be calm. Be firm. Be patient. Clarity will prevail with time

43. Stillness of mind should not stagnate you

44. Moments may be clouded or dark. You always have the spark

45. Search for inner peace will blossom if you start respecting yourself

46. Do not sleep for too long and be part of the wake

47. Grudges are like droplets trapped in layers of memories. They have the power to make you weep

48. Silent in the moment will seize the words

49. Smudge the rigidness to ease your life

50. You deserve to experience Brewtiful Morningszz with a cup filled with enthusiasm, love and zeal

Self-Awareness, Self-Respect and Integrity

Quotes about self-respect, integrity, understanding oneself and staying true to values.

1. Respect your reputable mind
2. Believe your beautiful heart
3. Value your valuable time
4. Oxygen is the source of life. Be accountable
5. Oxygen is the only ingredient for survival. Be responsible
6. Oxygen is a must for existence. Be respectful
7. Respect for others is a gifted trait no matter how unique we are
8. Accepting others in harmony is a mighty quality
9. Be humble and grounded
10. Power to glow is within you
11. Glow with your knowledge
12. Body shaming others reflects your own insecurities
13. Comparison with others will drift you away from your goals

14. Overthinking may lower your self-confidence

15. Neighbours are an asset. Be precious for them

16. Family is a bond by default. Don't try to find faults in them

17. Friends are there for a reason. Be a valuable one for them

18. Cousins are like gems in a memory box. Connect and make them rich

19. Dream should not mean you make no plans. It just means believe and you can

20. Knowledge does not mean you stop with degrees. It means you are a source of light for others

21. Confusion does not mean you don't have direction; it just means you are blessed with options

22. Sincerity does not mean perfection; it is the reason why you start

23. No matter how sharp you look, have a firm grip

24. Learn to value yourself. Don't pounce on every trivial bait

25. Your moments are waiting for your presence; make them awesome

26. Mark your territory. Boundaries are for small goals

27. Decisions mean responsibility! Value yourself

28. Do not be a prey to the fine web. Set your priorities

29. You forgive on the basis of your choice; are you really just?

30. Do not trap yourself in a cell

31. Unseen weight is at times heavier

32. Living in the moment is everything. It is the preview of your future memories

33. Memories are a collection of moments you are spending right now

34. The weight of your past can make you trudge

35. Lifting the weight of every word uttered will weigh you down

36. Grief is painful. Just because you can't see it doesn't mean it's not there

37. Trusting yourself no matter what happens is real you

38. Clear up the folds in your mind and let your heart beat with a new rhythm

39. A sludge of emotions will slowly pile up if you hold onto your hurt or anger for too long

40. Attitudes are contagious. Make yours worth catching

Vision, Growth and Opportunity

Quotes about vision, seizing opportunities, personal growth and long-term success.

1. There is light beyond clouded vision
2. Hope is like oxygen to our mind
3. Want – an unknown feeling of need within your perceived comfort zone
4. Wish – thought in the future without knowing its impact
5. We are just a speck in this universe. Live your life and spread joy to create a happy storm
6. Life will be vibrant if you hold your passion in fashion
7. Every opportunity in life is some form of signal
8. You are the CEO of your life
9. Follow the rules and your path will be regulated
10. Your trajectory of grit will take you to places
11. With every passing moment, our memory has the power to wash away heavy sighs
12. Everything can be in harmony and peace. Time to live the moments you seize
13. Your path may be meandering. But you will have an impact. Realise your potential

14. Before you start your journey, be sure you are on the right track

15. Do not procrastinate. Hunt your goals

16. Celebrate together from wherever!

17. Opportunities flow if you know when to budge

18. The right direction and efforts will take you to places you rightly deserve

19. The pain ingrained in time loses its power once grit shines in the eyes

20. Keep life Simply Complicated

21. We can be in clusters with the same situations. Our identity to grow as an individual is retained

22. It's time to Quit worrying. Join hundreds of others who are hoping to kick the habit!

23. Assemble your energies to make an impact!

24. You always have the key to light your way

25. Life is a game no matter what shadows befall on your ground. Just hang around! Play with your skills and surprise yourself

26. Your phones are charged. How about you?

27. Nudge your path with light, hope and positivity

28. Sometimes in life hurdles can protect you

29. Any form of light that lights your vision will brighten the dark moments

30. No matter what your stature, remember to be rooted firmly

31. Think before you sink

32. Choose your colour carefully and let your true self shine

33. The music of your life is in the rhythm of your heart

34. Live in the moment and be free from all the unwanted grids that have caged you

35. The warmth of virtual glare can never match the real one. Organise and step out

36. Connect with warmth however frigid your surroundings

37. Relive your passion. Do not let the moments stagnate

38. Your looks may be unique. But your skills will make an impact

39. Your attitude will help you to stand out without any doubt

40. No matter what's your growth, you still need time with yourself

Parting Thoughts

As you reflect on these quotes, it's essential to remember that life is a journey – a continuous flow of moments, experiences and opportunities for growth. Each day offers a chance to strengthen your clarity, deepen your resilience and expand your understanding of who you are and who you are becoming.

We often spend our time striving, comparing and seeking perfection. Yet, the true magic of life happens when we embrace the ebb and flow of each moment, with patience, determination and a positive mindset. The journey is not always about the destination, but about how we move forward and grow with each step we take.

Your path is yours to create. You have the power to shape it with your thoughts, actions and mindset. The challenges you face are opportunities to grow stronger, and the people you meet are mirrors reflecting lessons you can learn. Embrace every part of your journey, knowing that you are always evolving, always capable and always worthy of the dreams you seek.

Take a moment today to ask yourself: What can I do to live more fully in the present moment and continue growing towards the person I aspire to be?